KHAMRIYYAT HONG KONG

KHAMRIYYAT HONG KONG

Resource Publications
An Imprint of Wipf and Stock Publishers
199 W. 8th Ave., Suite 3
Eugene, OR 97401

www.wipfandstock.com

PAPERBACK ISBN: 979-8-3852-5298-5
HARDCOVER ISBN: 979-8-3852-5299-2
EBOOK ISBN: 979-8-3852-5300-5

08/04/25

KHAMRIYYAT HONG KONG

AHMED ELBESHLAWY
Foreword by Alan Jefferies

RESOURCE *Publications* • Eugene, Oregon

R

One should always be drunk. That's all that matters; that's our one imperative need. So as not to feel Time's horrible burden that breaks your shoulders and bows you down, you must get drunk without ceasing.

But what with? With wine, with poetry, or with virtue, as you choose. But get drunk.

And if, at some time, on the steps of a palace, in the green grass of a ditch, in the bleak solitude of your room, you are waking up when drunkenness has already abated, ask the wind, the wave, a star, the clock, all that which flees, all that which groans, all that which rolls, all that which sings, all that which speaks, ask them what time it is; and the wind, the wave, the star, the bird, the clock will reply: ‹It is time to get drunk! So that you may not be the martyred slaves of Time, get drunk; get drunk, and never pause for rest! With wine, with poetry, or with virtue, as you choose!›

—CHARLES BAUDELAIRE

Contents

Foreword by Alan Jefferies xiii
Acknowledgments xvii
Author's Introduction xix

City, Space, and Committee 1
Two Men 2
Blood Knowledge 4
Remembrance 5
January 13th 6
Amidst Thorns 7
Rick's Cafe 8
To Poets 10
Unconcerned Onlooker 11
Managers 13
She's Chinese 15
Catch Him 17
Books on a Bed, or, Carcass on a Bed II 18
The Right 19
Recurring Vision 20
Pain 21
Bees in Trouble 22
Loving Your Mother 23
Somebody 24
American Friend and American Poet 25
A Lesson at the Dawn of Civilization 26

Contents

I am a Writer 27
Judaic Lesson 28
Gaze 30
In Gaza 31
Worn-out Book 33
Anthony on Octavius, or Vice Versa 34
Half-hidden Smiles 35
Before Hell's Gate 36
Reciting Poetry 38
Sandy Eyes II 39
Priorities 41
On Suella Braverman 43
A Hong Kong Lady 44
When I can't Write in the Presence of Beauty 46
America 47
The Incident 49
Singing 51
Incarnation 53
Stories 54
Christ Remembering What Happened In Judea 55
Reduction 56
Plight 58
Song 59
God 61
Purity 63
Roma Rosso 64
An Advice to My Religious Friend 66
Debt 67
Heaven 68
Honest Statement 69
Car 70
The Grotesque 72
Gwei-lo 74
Poetic Selfishness 76
The Students 77
An Old Oak 78

Meeting May 80

Love 82

Feeling 84

My Shadow 85

January 13th . . . Again 86

The Perfectionist 88

Old Prostitutes 89

Solitary Figure 91

Saint 93

Unaccepted 94

Lost Time 95

Simple Beings 96

Without You 98

Wine, Woman, and Pen 99

Red Wine Discourse 100

Women and the Muslim Tradition 101

Gaza 103

You and I 104

Guilt 105

The Problem 106

One of us is mistaken 108

Liquid 109

Lullaby 110

Recommended Readings, Films, and Operas 111

Foreword

THE POETIC VOICE THAT emerges from Ahmed Elbeshlawy's latest collection "Khamriyyat Hong Kong" is one that is strong, direct and most of all longing for connection. It is a voice that has travelled from his homeland in Egypt to his adopted home of China; more specifically, the hubbub of Hong Kong with its skyscrapers and neon canyons. An unlikely destination for a poet one might think. Yet, as we know the poet's journey is always surprising, and the fruits, likewise enlivening and unexpected.

It's a question the poet seems to ask himself in his poem "Feeling":

> *"Hong Kong—*
> *How did that happen and why?*
> *I can't speak Cantonese*
> *After so many years*
> *In this beloved and alienating place*
> *Why did you open your arms*
> *So wide for me?*

The poem ends:

> *I lost my virginity to you,*
> *To the point of no return;*
> *To the point of not knowing who*
> *You are, or who I am anymore.*
> *Like Alexandria to Cavafy,*
> *You've become pure feeling for me.*

"Feeling"

An astute observer of people and places—a flaneur in the tradition of Baudelaire—it's almost as if Ahmed's powers of observation have been sharpened by his status as an "outsider"—a poet from elsewhere. In the poem "Gwei-lo", for example, he plays with the idea of being other than white and other than Chinese in what is an overwhelmingly a Chinese city:

> *"To be one of the 'ghost people'*
> *Who doesn't want to be a white devil*
> *When white devils seem too happy*
> *In their white devilishness"*

The poet goes on to guiltily admit to feeling somewhat privileged to be referred—albeit briefly—by the common Hong Kong slur.

In the poem "An Old Oak" Elbeshlawy beautifully draws a very human portrayal:

> *Her wrinkled hands*
> *Cupped the cup firmly*
> *While rubbing thoroughly*
> *With soap rinsing it.*
> *All traces of coffee were gone.*
> *The old face smiled at me*
> *Triumphantly—*
> *The simple job was done.*

This sense of being an outsider—a "passionate spectator" as Baudelaire puts it—permeates much the work. The poet's reaction to this somewhat confusing place varies within each poem and throughout the entire collection. Poems of love, confusion, astonishment and often observed with a certain wry sense of humor.

My favorite poem in this vein is "Incident." The entire poem is basically a dialogue between the poet and a member of the famed Hong Kong Constabulary who is attempting to gather information about an undisclosed incident. The contrast between the hyper-efficiency of the police officer and the laconic devil-may-care responses of the poet speaks volumes about the different cultural responses to authority.

As the title of this collection and the author's introduction makes clear one of the main themes of this book is imbibing; boozing—and you'll certainly find those poems here:

> *Ideas come to him*
> *Harrowing*
> *Only when he's drunk—*
> *They can't come when*
> *He's too entangled in*
> *The million banal things*
> *That fill his daily life*

"Singing"

Wine, the poet says loosens inhibitions and facilitates truth telling. *In vino veritas*—in wine, there is truth, the ancient Romans remind us.

One time where the poet's passion most definitely overwhelms the innate spectator is in the poems dealing with the suffering of his beloved Palestinian people. On this topic strong views and raw emotions are set forth and Elbeshlawy doesn't hold back—condemning both sides.

> *Children, wait for us*
> *In the darkness of death!*
> *We're on our way too,*
> *Like all the things*
> *That are to die.*
>
> *The difference though*
> *Is that you were lucky*
> *Enough not to live long*
> *And witness our collective*
> *Conspiratorial cowardice.*
>
> *Here's a lullaby*
> *To help you sleep peacefully:*

"Lullaby"

His sympathies though are always with the innocents caught between the sides of what appears increasingly to be an endless conflict.

In conclusion, this collection of poems comes highly recommended. Within it you will find the work of a poet at the height of his powers. An assured, direct, perceptive and at times raw poetic voice; willing to put everything on-the-line for his vocation.

Alan Jefferies,
poet and children's author

Alan Jefferies was born in Brisbane and raised in Quandamooka Country, the Redlands. He started writing in high school and publishing after moving to Sydney in the mid-seventies. Between 1998 and 2007 he lived and worked in Hong Kong where he co-founded (with Mani Rao and Kit Kelen) OutLoud; Hong Kong's longest running English language poetry reading. He's published six books of poetry, his most recent being "in the same breath" (Flying Islands, 2021). He currently lives on Macleay Island, in the state of Queensland.

Acknowledgments

I AM GRATEFUL TO Alan Jefferies for his close reading of the poems of *Khamriyyat Hong Kong* and the insightful foreword that he wrote to this collection. I would also like to thank C. J. Anderson-Wu, Akin Jeje, and Azam Abidov for reading the *Khamriyyat* and writing advance comments on the work.

Three poems from *Khamriyyat Hong Kong,* namely, "The Incident," "Worn-out Book," and "Bees in Trouble" appeared before in different issues of Taiwan&Masticadores online poetry magazine. My thanks go to its Editor, C. J. Anderson-Wu. Five other poems, namely, "Rick's Café," "To Poets," "Unconcerned Onlooker," "Managers," and "She's Chinese" are scheduled to appear in *Nadwah* poetry magazine. My thanks go to *Nadwah's* Editor, Dr. Sayed Gouda.

Finally yet importantly, I would like to thank my favorite artist, Ms. Malak Elbeshlawy, for designing the front cover of *Khamriyyat Hong Kong.*

Author's Introduction

IN ARABIC, KHAMRIYYAT MEANS 'wine poems'—poems about wine, or, poems written under the effect of wine. The connection between wine and poetic creativity needs no explanation to poets who happen to drink wine, or wine lovers who happen to write poetry. For poets and poetry readers who do not drink wine, and wine lovers who do not read or write poetry, a little clarification may be useful.

Wine eliminates pretense; it makes one face his/her own thoughts without the ideological sieve, just like making love as a basic instinct without having to enact the niceties and the tact that precedes it. Wine seems to make the subject go straight towards what is irking him/her without having to bother with side issues. Moreover, it makes the mind linger on descriptive details—essential to poetry—that it cannot possibly tolerate when it is in a sober state.

Most importantly, wine makes the drunken poet love himself or herself enough to think that what they need to put down on paper is actually important for others to know—even if it is not. It seems to reduce hours of thought; that is to say thought which is often seriously hindered by lots of linguistic signs that try to hold the writer back and reign him/her in. Wine takes writers where they do not usually go because of fear, anxiety, political correctness, or just habit.

Writing under the effect of wine may not reveal any truth, but it makes the writer knock relentlessly on the door behind which truth keeps hiding herself—knowing too well that it will never open. Wine does not end suffering life, but it makes people enjoy the suffering endlessly. Thus, writing poetry under the effect of wine is less about producing anything than it is about enjoying the act of writing. With wine, the journey is always more enjoyable than reaching any destination.

It remains to say that in the middle of writing the Khamriyyat, during a phase of relative self-contentment and peace of mind, Harakat al-Muqawamah al-Islamiyyah (Islamic Resistance Movement), or, Hamas attacked Israel in an unprecedented way and took hundreds of Israeli civilians as hostages. Israel responded by committing the largest genocide in its Zionist history killing thousands of civilian men, women, and children in Gaza.

Inevitably, a few of my Khamriyyat quickly turned sour, angry, and much more political than I intended them to be. Those fascist killers, on both sides, inadvertently managed to disrupt the state of tranquility during which I was writing my Khamriyyat. I am not sure whether this was good or bad though, as poetry still came out of that disruption.

City, Space, and Committee

We can't publish the words of this poet;
He is too painfully honest
For a city that always lived under cover.

He tends to reduce the distance
Between our naked bodies and that
Wall to zero millimeters.

The wall feels good, we have to admit,
But, there's too much spotlight,
And, as the sage once said,

Everyone knows too well what happens
When you catch the truth naked at night
Against a wall—and that's all.

We can't publish the words of this poet.

Two Men

(inspired by my old and messy personal library)

"Spectacle is the sun that never sets over the empire of modern passivity."
—*GUY DEBORD, THE SOCIETY OF THE SPECTACLE*

Two men;
One reads too well
And creates
To fill the gap
Of his need
To consume people,
The other toils
Endlessly
For other people
Just to make
Ends meet.
They meet,
Occasionally,
Under Debord's
Omnipresent sun.
They don't make sense
To each other.
They're born of
The same mother.

They know deep inside
That they are one,
That they are none,
That they're tired,
And that they're done.

Blood Knowledge

It may appear easy
To write what you feel
Without passing it by
The sieve of rational thinking.
Yet the ability to conceive
Something
That moves directly
From one blood stream to another
Isn't what it seems
In the world of elite letters.
This is the blood knowledge
Of inexplicable poesy.
And, it isn't for he
Who puts his mind apart
From the body's tangibility,
Nor for the faint at heart.

Remembrance

Yes,
I do remember—
No,
I cannot talk.
Gone
Is that light.
Hush!
It's just a number
Now,
Covered in smoke—
Shun
The brave night!
Dark
I have become—
Pretending
To be 'happy',
Imagining
That I still am
The city of light.

January 13th

It is this time of the year—
The world is desolate,
Again.

13 January—
The umbilical cord—
Cut.

Unconditional love—
No more—
No obituary—

First life—
Over.
Now, just exposed

To the elements
On your own—
No cover—

The Tristan Chord—
The naked knife—
God.

Amidst Thorns

In a colourless coppice where poison thrives
In a lattice writhed of venomous vines,
Crowned with thistles of toxic pride,
And thorned guardians clutch their spines,
There blooms a heart no curse can claim—
A sylvan flower none dare to name.
Its petals part the festered air,
With a sapphire sigh, brave and rare.
The coppice, though choked on bitter dew,
Bends close and questions the hue:
"Who dares to defy our black reign?"
The flower raises its head to explain
With a beauty that wears no armour;
It breathes where all else turns to ache,
Like a star no darkness can truly take.

Rick's Cafe

Paula had a small fashion shop,
An extremely nervous fluffy cat,
And a cross-eyed muscular man
Who visited her frequently,
And who looked menacing to me
Every time I saw him in the lift,
Until I knew, one day, that his name was just Bob.

If not for Paula and Bob,
I wouldn't have been allowed
To enter Rick's Café
In the 1996 HK,
For there were two big white men
At the gate
Who made it look quite Kafkaesque.

I saw them preventing people with dark skin
From stepping in.
To date, I still wonder what
Exactly took place
At that moment of trance
About ten meters away
From the guarded entrance.

The gory guards magically stepped aside,
And I got in—
Firmly flanked by a frowning Paula
And a feisty ready-to-fight Bob.
Once in, however,
I realized there were enough people
Of every possible color.

Everyone was drinking,
Everyone was swaying to the music,
Everyone was kissing
Someone else.
So, I turned to Paula and said:
"Hey! This place looks great!"
She said, "Yes, racism is only at the gate."

To Poets

When a poem is born,
Watch out!

When it creates its world
In hypnotic words,

An instance of life
Has aged enough

To die in words,
So, watch out!

For that instance
Cannot be revived

By any words—
It can only be a memory.

The dawn of a poem emerges
At the dusk of life.

When a poem is born,
Watch out!

Unconcerned Onlooker

You should save me
From this mumbling
Behind the partition.
You should save me
From drunkenness.

Where are the ethics
Of Confucianism?
Where are the manners
Of Japanese people?
Aren't you the half-Chinese
Half-Japanese hybrid
Creation of Asian civilization?

I am uncivilized;
I am a modern Egyptian
Who has nothing to do
With the old glory.
I am a Muslim
Who has everything to do
With the current shit.

I am dark-skinned
I am dangerous
I am damned.
I am the devil himself.

Nevertheless, I've been told
That you are lotus blossom
Who takes the damned
In her bosom.

What? Am I mistaken?
Did they lie to me about that too?

Damn that lying creature!
Damn literature!

Managers

It is becoming difficult
To determine where and why
The words were written—
On a small paper—
On a computer—
On the cellular—
On which account?
Which application?
There are just too many—
And a lot of passwords.
What do the words
Mean now anyway?

It is not exactly practical
To go back to the good old
Notebook and the pen—
They aren't always ready—
Some other tools
Gained ground on them
And, to my hand
Became closer.

In the future
Everybody will need a manager—
To manage the accounts—
And the managers will need managers
Who will need other managers.

One day, Everyone
Will be managing
Someone else's life—
Until we all forget
Who is managing what;

We will be
Kafkaesque couriers—
Carrying a lot of messages
Around that can never be delivered
To anyone—

Because everyone,
Eventually, in time,
Will be the sender and receiver
Of his own message—
Which never left him

That will be
The sad and silent
End of the world.

She's Chinese

I imposed something on her—
A certain position,
A certain course,
Certain terms of reference.

Now, she feels that she has
To impose something on me
In return—it's only fair.
You see? She's Chinese—
Very much so,
And she won't simply let it go.

I wonder where that comes from—
This urge to get even;
Not prevalent, not victorious,
But simply on the same ground.

After almost thirty years
In this confusing and confused city
I still don't quite get it.
It has become pure feeling for me—
Just like Alexandria to Cavafy.

I look at her, perplexed,
And she looks back at me
In bewilderment—
As if I should by now understand
What she means.

But, I don't.

Catch Him

The drunken man
Is more responsible;
He attends to meticulous details,
He is clear about boundaries and principles,
He is much more compassionate,
Much more generous with everything
And everyone, much more accepting
and approving of others,

Much more able to analyze;

The drunken man
Is much more generous
even with his feelings and smiles
He just loves other creatures
Whoever and whatever they are;
He acknowledges the sublimity of their creator
Without seeing or knowing him.

Catch him before he gets sober!
Witness his humanity and weakness
Before he becomes calculative and afraid—
Again!

Books on a Bed, or, Carcass on a Bed II

My books are on her bed—
Finally.
My life's work,
The only
Real achievement I made
For myself.

I am in her bed
In terms of the important
Things that I have said—
So loudly,
Yet so silently,
Mainly to myself.

She made sure
To photograph
The books on the bed;
She made sure
To give me
That little pleasure,

And that was indeed
Generous of her,
For she knew that,
By any measure,
That was as close as I can get
To that bed.

The Right

Consider me
Pessimistic,
But,
Whoever has the money
Has the right.
And don't ask what right.
It is just the right.
And you know what I mean
So,
Don't pretend
That you don't know.

Recurring Vision

Night.
Awake.
Heavy sigh;
Too heavy to move.
A crowd of illusions
On the walls.
Same time,
The past returns—
The present fades away,
As the wind moans
Past the window
And the bewildered air
Plays the golden hair
While my wounds wail.
Oh, dawn, come!

Pain

Your grim gripping griping ghastly madness
Finally got to us.
The scratchy snatchy spasmodic siren's scream
Silenced my love.
And there you are, my love,
The dedicated dutiful devoted doting dove
Desiring a divorce.

Who'd have thought those twenty years of love
Will go down the drain
Just because I forgot what you said
A few minutes ago about
One of the kids?
Forgive me, but I was just watching the rain
And thinking how to remain

In the realm of passion and prepossessing pain—
O yes, I never told you but
Pain was pleasant,
Pain was pleasurable,
Pain was perfect.
Pain colored our dreams, and when we lost it,
We were left with the meaningless screams.

Bees in Trouble

A bee hummed and swung sharply from right to left. He has been looking all day long for a child to sting. "Where have all the little ones gone? What a waste of precious time! Can't one get done with his suicidal mission?"

He knew it wasn't exactly wise to find a child to immunize then drop dead on the spot. Yet, he kept looking for his certain death. But what was wrong with this town? The landscape wasn't changing. He seemed to buzz his way in the air from ruin to ruin.

Another bee came flying from the opposite direction. This one was screaming: "Get out of here! It's appalling! Some people are killing the children with mass murdering machines, and others are swearing they won't let any child to live peacefully in this town for a thousand years to come."

"What? Are you saying that we can't sting any children here? We can't have an honorable death?"

"No, my friend, not here. Honor departed from here. It is no country for young ones."

Loving Your Mother

Whisper 'safe trip' in her ear on my behalf!

Wish her good luck from a friend she never saw!

Give her a high five and a furtive little wink!

Tell her that blood knowledge is the only real knowledge!

Give her a light pinch on the arm, and be gentle with the wrinkled skin!

And make sure to show her you've got your own mark on yours!

Let her be assured that it runs in the family!

Let her know that you follow with a sense of duty and commitment!

Give her a new life and a renewed enjoyment!

Let her know that old age can be fun!

Let her know that she can be dwarfed by none!

Give her a sip of your red wine, and tell her what you're going to do after!

Light and smoke a cigarette together!

Let her know the friend is an incarnation of her lover!

Take care of your mother! Take good care of your mother!

Somebody

Oh, yes, there are boundaries—
Ethical ones,
Whether you like them or not.
They appear at the horizon
Of another tangible body
And you cannot be nobody;

You must be somebody,
Even if you think
That you don't qualify—
Especially when you think
That you don't qualify.

Haven't you heard?
It is only those who can afford it
Who can be truly anonymous.
But you can't be anonymous.
You must have a proper name,
And your name
Is your cross.

So, if you are short on cash,
Just get crucified,
And, enjoy it!
Like Jesus.

American Friend and American Poet

My American friend, who's as fond
Of Shiraz Cabernet as I am,
Stopped writing to me,
Suddenly.
At first, he sympathized.
Who wouldn't sympathize with
Children whose only fault was
That they were born on a stolen land
That is theirs and not theirs?
Then I guess he just got tired—
After all, it has become a norm
To read about children being targeted
By war planes and 2,000-pound bombs.
Now I understand what the wise
Drunken American poet meant when he wrote
That "the trouble with these people is
That their cities have never been bombed,
And their mothers have never been told to shut up."

A Lesson at the Dawn of Civilization

Did you take it as a joke
When I told you to take
Care of the girls, Stoic?

It wasn't at all a joke.

We're supposed to take
Care of our women for God's sake!
We must protect them,

Mind you what I say,

If necessary, with our lives.
'Our women' means mothers,
Sisters, wives, and daughters.

And, this has nothing to do

With honor, my dear son;
Don't you ever listen again
To the damned oracle priests!

It's for our survival.

I am a Writer

That is to say,
The plumber
Is better than me,
And definitely,
More useful—

The physician,
The architect,
The teacher,
The seamstress,
The domestic helper,

The garbage man,
The prostitute;
They're all more useful
Than me.
What keeps me thankful

Is that I think I am still better
Than a politician.

Judaic Lesson

for both Zionists and Islamists
(who surely won't understand it, but normal people will)

I picked out his "Aesthetic Theory" again after so many years. Upon reading a few lines, the old and bald man himself was sitting in front of me. He smiled. "Do you consider yourself American or German?" I asked him. "I have never been an American. I couldn't. I didn't even try," he said in a distinctive German American accent. "Would you like to watch a movie?" I asked. He frowned. "No, no, it isn't what you think," I said quickly, recalling his thoughts about what cinema is, "this film is a celebrated comedy-drama about a Jewish man who uses his imagination to protect his son from the horrors of internment in a Nazi concentration camp. It's called "La vita è bella," and it has the power to make you cry while you're laughing and laugh while you're crying and . . ." "Stop!" he interrupted with his two palms in the air, "I totally reject the idea of laughter about such a matter. Auschwitz cannot be joked about in any sense." "Oh, I am sorry," I said, "I forgot that you did write about that even before the birth of the idea."

Then I remembered Wagner. I know that he developed a strongly critical perspective on Wagner's music, which he associated with the emergence of fascism. I wanted to provoke him again and watch his reaction. "Would you like to listen to Wagner? I love him. I have all four operas of "Der Ring des Nibelungen." He laughed and said, "Now it is just too obvious that you're trying to aggravate me on purpose. It isn't working." We both laughed. I just love this man, I thought. I'm truly contented that he died more than half a century ago before he could witness how many of his own people ended up being more fascist than their oppressors.

I wanted to show him that I would sacrifice some of the things I truly love in honor of his thought and his "Aesthetic Theory." I brought all the Blu-ray discs carrying "La vita è bella" and "Der Ring des Nibelungen," put them on the table in front of him, then I brought my big kitchen gas lighter and said: "I will send both Benigni and Wagner to Hell right now. Do you know why? Because the truth is, you're much more important to me than both of them." I lighted the gun. At this point, his face turned crimson red. He threw both of his arms around the discs making a barrier between them and the flame like his own neck was under a guillotine. Then, as if he couldn't even believe what he was witnessing, he screamed at the top of his voice, in burning rage, in German: "Nicht berühren! Das ist Kunst!"

Gaze

It was highly intimate
Like creating a work of art,
A painting
Of two naked bodies
Touching
Each other
Under the gaze
Of the painter
Who wanted nothing
But relation—
To be part
Of his creation.

In Gaza

In Gaza,
There's only Man per se,
At the zero level of humanity—
And that means all of us—

Naked, exposed, vulnerable and
Without any qualifications.

You can go and read your Bible,
Your Qur'an, and your Talmud
For as long as you want.

You can be educated, sophisticated,
Knowledgeable to the level of arrogance,

Like Solomon,

Chosen by no less than God
Himself, but, if you can't get
Yourself to identify with that
Absolute zero level of humanity,

In Gaza,

Then know that you're nothing
But a sorry product of something else;

It can be capitalism, Zionism,
Fundamentalism, ism, ism, ism,

Social media, plastic surgery,
Cloning, clowning, climbing—

You name it.
But it can't be humanity.

Worn-out Book

Watch out
For the comradely feeling
You get when you flip
The yellow pages
Of a worn-out book
Read by strangers
Who are now friends
In a peculiar way
Through touching
The same old papers—
Watch out!

Love is always about
Seeing in people
What's more than people;
The written word,
Literature,
Cast on a forehead
After it was read
On the yellow pages
With so many eyes
To the point of becoming
Worn-out.

Anthony on Octavius, or Vice Versa

Let the boy talk
As much as he wants
About great Rome and her fortunes.

It won't affect—
In the world of men—
The notion that the happiest

Moment of all
Is that dear moment
Of unconditional entrance.

Half-hidden Smiles

There can't be anything beyond
The smile now behind the mask.
The smile is a kind of promise to come back
To life and love once this pandemic
Decides to go away.

We've learnt that distancing
May be the most difficult
Thing to abide by.

It did help reading and writing
As a convenient compensation
For consuming bodies,
Or at least for showing respect
By a simple caress.

Out of the half-hidden smiles
I wrote a whole book of poems—
Each is a replacement for a missed kiss.

Before Hell's Gate

Yes,
I did spend my whole life
Chasing an illusory mirage.

What?
Are you telling me that
You were able to catch yours?

Odd!
I thought we're all alike
In failing to be lucky and large.

Shit!
So some people did
Succeed in the bloody farce.

God,
Are you going to let
Them get away with that?

What?
I am the bad guy
With the envious evil eye?

Wait!

Wait!

Hot!

Hot!

Hot!

Reciting Poetry

I cannot recite my own words
Without shaking, without wild nervousness,
Or without deadening my body a bit with wine;

It's bad enough to have written
Those truthful but strange words in the first place
For searching eyes and suspicious minds that aren't mine;

It's bad enough to be smitten
By the merciless sword of otherness—
The tenacious gaze sending a shiver down my spine;

It is bad enough that those words
Seem to emerge from beyond awareness,
Whipping no one but their sayer with a cat o' nine.

Sandy Eyes II

Last night I dreamt
Of her sandy eyes again;

The first glass of red
Wine, by some miracle,
Spilled over the checkered
Skirt of the long bridge
As she murmured
Some soothing words
To ease the sense
Of loss, the certain tinge
That I was robbed
And beaten to death
Long before being distracted
By too much reading
Leading to this crack
In the wall through which
I just looked, loved, and ditched
Like a broken machine beyond
Repair, beyond saving, and
Beyond producing anything
But senseless repetition.

Hungry dogs kept barking
Around the kitchen table
Across which she stretched
Her arms playfully and
Offered her stingy hands—
Smilingly too—
The barking woke me up.

Priorities

Just to keep records,
Priorities changed
After the 6th bottle of beer;

I must apologize
To that masseuse—
I crossed my line.

I have to tell my wife, today,
That without her,
I'd have been dead years ago.

I must give wet food
To my adorable cat, tonight;
She's been on dry food for two days.

I must call all of my relatives,
One by one, to say hello
And chat about nothing—

Just to keep connection
With the vagina,
As Islam teaches.

I must smile when I see my boss
Tomorrow; She's not really as bad
As I usually think she is.

I must make peace,
Immediately, With people,
And with God.

I should be satisfied
With what I have,
Because I have a lot.

See? The happy Christmas reindeer
Only starts to show up
After the sixth bottle of beer.

On Suella Braverman

Poor Suella—
She tried to prove
That she's whiter than the white,
Far-righter than the far right,
More Israeli than the Israelite,
And more Zionist than the Zionist.
It didn't work.

A Hong Kong Lady

Thank God
She finally bent down
To pick up the two-dollar coin
That she dropped
After almost a whole minute
Of going through her handbag
Looking for God knows what.
The old man
Who kicked back the coin
In her direction,
In a purely reflexive action,
Is also smiling happily—
Everything is in order.
The minute was quite long;
The face, long,
The frown, menacing,
The hand movements
Inside the bag, mad,
The mind racing:
'Bend down?!
For a two-dollar coin?!
That he kicked back?!
With his old shoe?!
In front of all the others too?!'
Everyone around
Was waiting . . .
Until she made

The courageous decision
To bend down and
Pick the goddamn thing
Casually,
Like doing something
On the side.
It is only in Hong Kong
That such a simple deed
Looks like suicide.

When I can't Write in the Presence of Beauty

It is scary—
Absolutely frightening;
Beauty comes in,
Glowing,
Yet, I feel nothing.

The white page
Seems to stare
Back at me,
Challenging the wine,
Even though
The willowy doe
Isn't mine—

I just keep tapping
With this impatient pen
On the table—
A frowning monkey god
Who is unable
To create anything—
In solitude—
No defiant son,
No Mary.

It is scary.

America

I always wanted her;
I still want her;
The East Coast and
Edward Said,
The West Coast and
Charles Bukowski,
The Mid-West and
Ihab Hassan;
The ferret that ran
Across the street
Upon seeing me,
The Hollywood sign
On Mount Lee,
The cinematic society
That escapes reality endlessly,
The broad smile
Which doesn't mean anything,
The perfect white teeth
That Baudrillard noticed,
The empty streets
That seem more menacing
Than the old crowded subway stations,
The boy with the big doll
Strolling down the street,
The inexplicably long
Black limousine,
The man who wanted money

Just for giving me directions,
The black man who dramatized
The history of the British ship
To make the tourists laugh,
The Latina Officer at the airport
Who wanted to fuck me—
America—
The innocent woman
Who sucks everyone in.
America—
The Statue of Liberty
That smirks furtively
As you get in,
Unaware of the invisible sword
That cuts your private parts
And throw them in a bin.
America—
God's land par excellence,
God's hell par excellence,
And God's resting place
Par excellence.
Don't fool yourself;
Don't imagine that it will simply wane
One day;
When she dies,
Everyone will.

The Incident

The interrogator asked:
"Did you witness the incident?"

"No," I said.

"Did you hear about it?"

"No, no one told me."

"Did you notice that the lady
Was very angry that morning?"

"She's always angry in the morning."

"Did you hear her shouting 'asshole'
At the top of her lungs at the man?"

"No, I didn't, but he does look like one."

"How is that?"

"He never said 'good morning' to me."

The interrogator's eyes widened.

"So, you think he's an asshole because
He never greeted you in the morning?"

"Yes, that is what I think."

"Do you know what the lady claims he did to her?"

"Not really, but I can listen."

The interrogator's eyes widened again.

Then he made a dismissing hand gesture
To his colleague and said: "gweilo."

He asked his last question:
"Where were you at 9:30 AM Tuesday last?"

"Probably checking porn websites
While having my morning coffee."

When the report came out it said:
"This man neither knows anything about the incident
Nor does he know anything about his colleagues."

Singing

Ideas come to him
Harrowing
Only when he's drunk—
They can't come when
He's too entangled in
The million banal things
That fill his daily life.

Politicians realized this
From the dawn
Of civilization—
They made sure to multiply
The daily banal things
For everybody else,
Lest they start

Drinking,
Thinking,
Writing,

And, God forbid,

Singing

The primitive songs
Of the naked man
Who was not afraid
Of the elements—

The man who thought
That he authored himself
And everything else
Around him.

Incarnation

She didn't know when or how
She fell in love with her torturer,
Even though the night visitor
Was unbelievably cruel.
He listened to Wagner—
So attentively—while gazing at her
Overworked body with an evil eye.
He had his vile doctors
Electrocuting her private parts.
Yet she, somehow, reached
Dark depths and dizzying heights
Of a shameful but powerful pleasure
She didn't even imagine
Can exist right in the midst
Of absolute humiliation.
Before she died in the camp,
She gave birth to a child
Who later fathered a new nation
Unconcerned about the hymn
Of the temple or the church bells—
A nation marching forward
Yet backward as well—
And in every other face, You find
A little Adolf. And in every other
Voice, an angry little Goebbels.

Stories

Everyone thinks that his story is special,
Everyone believes that his can be made into a film,
And we could all be right about just that,
But there are people among us who seem to be certain
That their stories are truly admired by something in the universe.
Those are dangerous people,
And they are dangerous mostly to themselves.
Love your story, for it's indeed special—
Only not special enough to anyone else.

Christ Remembering What Happened In Judea

Nobody knew that I was enjoying it—
The taste of my own sweat,
The sharp stones scourging my flesh,
The whips drawing lines of blood,
The sense of defiance to power to be power,
Absolute, inscrutable, a force that doesn't cower,
And me getting crushed under its merciless foot,
The bones breaking beneath my heavy load,
The faces, the screams, the teeth, the commotion,
The tongues wiping the lips in anticipation,
The body, already, in little pieces,
Expecting its ultimate fragmentation.
I am not different, only more focused,
More aware of my body, attentive to its needs.
One thing frightened me beyond description,
That I should lose consciousness,
Lose the pain, lose the passion.
Preaching freaks, the lesson wasn't sacrifice,
It was enjoyment, it was my own anxiety,
My eyes witnessing my body's ultimate moment of piety.
That was the crucifixion—
This is what you repressed in your fiction.
And now that you know, will you stop insulting me
And cease singing my arrogant generosity in a choir?
The real faith, if you care to face
Yourselves in a mirror, your charted destiny,
Is that I lived and died according to my desire—
I wasn't saving you from hellfire.

Reduction

The cycle
Always went back to writing;
The fighting,
The women, the drinking,
The drowning in the dreary office
In dull deliberations
Over the year's target
Always ended
In nothing but writing.

The endless
Sheets of showing workaholic
Activity always disappeared
So easily
In the shadow of writing.

The fundamental need
For people
To talk to, to love,
To fume, to consume,
Always paved the way
To meet the beautiful blank
Paper that craved writing—
The pressure and the biting
Of the tip of this extremely
Sensual pen.

Nothing escaped
This uncanny economy
Of reducing the world
To the written word.

Plight

My father said:
"You belong to this family, and
In this family,
There are edicts to be followed."

My teacher said:
"You belong to this society, and
In this society,
There are traditions to be cherished."

The preacher said:
"you belong to this tribe, and
In this tribe,
There are strict laws to be obeyed."

It has always been difficult to fight
Being overwhelmed by the rules
Of family, society, and tribe.
The fight never led to anything but

Loneliness and fright.
Yet, at the end of the day,
No price is too high to pay
To be in such a sad but desirable plight.

Song

Don't be alarmed baby
When you see me
Stoned a little bit,
Stoned a little bit—
To forget the faces
Of the little children.
I am sorry but I am
Stoned a little bit,
Stoned a little bit,
To hide my fears,
To hide my tears,
Lest they know my weakness
Baby, and they won't
Have any mercy for me.
Excuse me love but
I am stoned a little bit,
Stoned a little bit,
To be able to deal with
Hearts made of stone,
To be able to smile
On Christmas Eve
In spite of all
The killings and the lies.
Forgive me dear
If I can't find my way
To my old laughs

Even though I am
Stoned a little bit,
Stoned a little bit,
For this is a different
Kind of a deadened body,
A different state of stone,
A different world,
A new page and a new stage
Of being with you,
Yet also being alone.

God

He tricked me into this
Because He could.
He knew everything,
And I didn't know anything.
He saw it all coming,
And I was blind.

He didn't ask me if
I wanted to go through it—
He just decided to throw me in.
May be He intended it
As a practical joke;
Maybe He just wanted
To have fun.

May be He thought
I would have fun too.
Well, I do, sometimes,
When I am drunk
And happen to be
With one of the beautiful
Creatures He created
And made sure to appropriate
For irresistible pleasures.

I just wonder what he wants—

To be thanked?
To be recognized?
To be worshipped?
Is this important to him?

Does He want me to shut up
And enjoy?
To close this awful mouth—
The disturbing harbinger
Of disturbing poetry—
And just bask In his mysterious light

And keep wondering?

Purity

I just can't understand
How can anyone today
Claim purity of race, blood,
Religion, or even thoughts.
In front of this huge
Corpus of literature
That we all have;
In front of the complex history,
And the endless chart
Of borrowed traditions,
Borrowed names,
Borrowed words,
And borrowed feelings,
How can one still claim
That he's one pure thing
Or another?
How can one still claim
That he's Jewish,
Or Christian, or Hindu,
Or Buddhist, or Muslim?
How can anyone claim
That he's not penetrated
By the Other?
And how come there are only
A handful of people
Who can see clearly
That claiming any purity
Is nothing but pure folly?

Roma Rosso

The waitress made a mistake
That day when she told me
Quietly that they will stop selling
The Italian Roma Rosso.
I shouted at her:
"Get your bloody bosso,
I have to talk to him or her
Right now!
This is irresponsible!
This specific red drink
Happens to be indispensable
To my writing of Hong Kong."

The man came
But he was too big to blame.
I told myself this is a time for reason.
"Do you know, good sir, what the world
Will be missing if you stop serving the Roma?
It will lose the good news,
The poetic prophecy made
In your establishment,
The very specific precious aroma,
The very essence of existence.
Can you imagine the world without the word?
And what will happen to civilization?
You tell me! You tell me!

The man was astounded—
Not by what I said
But by the inflated ego of the speaker.
Under the Rosso, I wasn't even the speaker.
He turned to the waitress
And said:
"Okay, now I really think
That it has become an urgent business
To stop serving this dangerous drink."

An Advice to My Religious Friend

To be ordinary
Is ordinary.
To think you're ordinary
Is the greatest iniquity
Against yourself,
Against humanity,
And against God.
So, instead of arrogance,
Try to be humble and fair;
Think that you are
Extraordinaire!
Like everyone else.

Debt

Those who are screwed,
Daily,
Do have a divine right
To collect the debt
Occasionally;
To screw someone
Every now and then.
If you don't believe me,
Ask Him.

Heaven

I dreamt that I woke up in heaven.
Everything was perfect;
The birds sang,
The palm trees swayed as drunken
Maidens in the wind,
The unimaginable women
Of legendary Eden
Came flocking to me,
Their only master,
The maestro of misk and disaster
And ceaseless love energy.
The rivers of wine and honey
Ran as wild as the ejaculated semen.
There was nothing more
To even dare
To imagine.
Yet, there was this hidden
But starkly present question:
When will something interesting
Ever happen?
Nietzsche was right after all;
"In heaven, all the interesting
People are missing."

Honest Statement

I am afraid you're misled;
It is not that we had our
Disagreements about
Certain little things
That finally made me
Unable to stand you.

The truth is that I am repelled
By the negative energy
And the strange smiling pout
Which somehow hinges
To that plumpy body
That is just so much you.

Car

I haven't forgotten you, 132;
The heavy hood I could hardly lift
With arms near noodle-thin,
The loose transmission that I feared,
The too-resistant clutch pedal
Thoroughly exhausting my boyish knee,
And that day of the first lessons
When the old man yelled at me:
"How many times must I repeat
That the one behind the wheel
Should always look forward
And not down at his damn feet?"
I remember my father's anger
With such a shaky youngster.
What memories you bring back,
Vehicle, what feelings you evoke!
And that tough body of yours
Which I deformed one unlucky day
Of my irresponsible youth,
Laying the blame on your old age,
And your unhurried response,
When the wise old man, in distress,
Stood up for you in candid defense—
"My dear, is this how you repay
Her for protecting your body with hers?"
O, shame on me! O, shame!
How ungrateful I was! How lame!

I stand today in front of you, 132,
After nearly forty years,
In nothing short of loving awe.

The Grotesque

We all love to see the grotesque.
Why would you stop on the highway
And lose precious time and risk
Missing your appointment
For a glimpse of fragmented bodies
That a collision spread away
If not for an unstoppable desire
To watch the suffering of others?
My Jewish friends are asking
Why I seem to be biased—
Why sympathize with the Palestinian
In the public domain
And not with the victim of October 7th?
The answer is simpler than
They think it is—
It seems to be . . .
My TV—
I saw the suffering body
Of the Palestinian—
I saw blood covering the faces
Of Palestinian children—
I didn't see the suffering body
Nor the frightened face of one
Israeli child, even though there must be
Some—hidden from the cameras.
It is about who has
The power of representation.

And I, simply, cannot identify with power.
If you can, feel free, my dear friend,
To survey the scene
From your ivory tower.

Gwei-lo

Gwei-lo—
Says the draft beer machine
In this old Hong Kong bar
Still serving mostly 'white devils.'

I'm not one of those by HK rules;
I'm just a particle of the brown sea
Extending from Bangladesh
To the west coast of Africa—

Listless, without an individual face,

Though I do remember
Being called gwei-lo just once
When the chatting movers realized
I can't communicate in Cantonese.

It felt like a privilege, of course,

To be one of the 'ghost people.'
Who doesn't want to be a white devil
When white devils seem too happy
In their white devilishness?

It always sounded playful anyway—
A smiling beautiful Asian mouth
Calling you 'gwei-lo', yes, a slur,
But a sexy one in its own way,

Like condemning someone meanly
While giving them a red rose
To sniff lustily like the devil they're—
Polite devils, yet somehow arrogant,

High ghosts, yet somehow low—

Gwei-lo,

Very, very gwei-lo.

Poetic Selfishness

It took me almost fifty years to scout
The ideas other people fought with
Across literature, and philosophy,

Only to know without a shred of doubt
That the only writers I'm in love with
Are the strange creatures called 'myself' and me.'

The Students

They just smiled and drank the blood of the children—
The Zionists, 'little Sunak' and 'senile Biden.'

American students couldn't continue to watch it—
Their country is now officially called

'The United States of Israel.'

Who changed its name? When? How? No one could tell.
But there is one thing that everyone knows too well;

Revolting students are ALWAYS right,
Even when they lose the fight.

An Old Oak

Her wrinkled hands
Cupped the cup firmly
While rubbing it thoroughly
With soap before rinsing it.
All traces of coffee were gone.
The old face smiled at me
Triumphantly—
The simple job was done.
She picked another cup
Casually.

I wonder how many hearts
Were broken
By her in her youth; how many
Touching love letters went up
In smoke
While she laughed heartily
At her lovers' folly—
Their desire to water
This particular oak—
Still so large in her old age.

There were no lovers now—
Just the silence of running water
Corroding skin
That simply didn't care
Anymore—
And the sulking of a satisfied soul
Inside a body that moved a lot
Only to prove
To a watchful community
That it was useful still.

She went on washing the cups
One by one—
Immersed in her inner world,
And the distant sounds
And colors of fading memories—
Oblivious to my attention
To her grace—
The godly space
That opened up to my eyes
By her old smiling face.

Meeting May

"Thanks for accepting my friend request,"
She wrote.
"Thank you," I wrote back.
"I am May, from Singapore, where
Are you from?"
"I am from Egypt. Do you like poetry?"
She ignored the question.
"The stock market is insane!
Do you play stocks?"

That is when I left the chat.

A few days later, she found me again
Somewhere else.
"Thanks for the connection!
I am May, from Singapore, where
Are you from?"
"I am from Hong Kong. Do you like Poetry?"
She ignored the question.
"The stock market is crazy!
Do you play stocks?"

"It doesn't matter, May,
Let me cut a long story short,
If I may;
I am not interested in the stock market,
I am only interested in poetry,
Red wine, and women.

She left the chat.

Social media taught us many lessons.
One of them is: hold your ground
And stick to your guns!

Love

We should not talk about love,
My love,
If you want it to go on.
It can't exist where it is a topic
For discussion.

You see? Once it is a subject,
I cease to be your lover—
I lose my particularity,
And anyone can fill in,
Literally, the gaping lack.

As long as we're outside language,
We can enjoy that as long as it lasts,
And it doesn't last long—
This is a song
That fades out

Before you can realize it's there;
Before reaching your ear.
We are supposed to have
What God ordained for us
Without questioning it.

So, let's not talk about love
And ruin what we have.
It means a lot to have something
In the first place,
For we are not gods,

We are just human beings
Who are doomed
To the temporality
Of everything
And everyone.

Feeling

Hong Kong—
How did that happen and why?
I can't speak Cantonese
After so many years
In this beloved and alienating place.
Why did you open your arms
So wide for me?
Why do you love foreignness
And isolate it at once?
How did you know about the lovers
Who can neither forget nor forgive
First love?
How did you know that some people
Aren't supposed to melt in?
Is this because you're yourself confused?
Is it because you cannot determine
Where the blood relation ends
And the sexual relation begins?
Is it because you don't remember
When you lost your virginity?
And to whom?
Or for whom?
I lost my virginity in you,
To the point of no return;
To the point of not knowing who
You are, or who I am anymore.
Like Alexandria to Cavafy,
You've become pure feeling for me.

My Shadow

How I wish to be just it—
Dark more by definition than nature,
Empty more by nature than definition,

Deeply simple without any depth,
Never existing in the dark,
Featureless, but with a clear outline,

Silent, but not subaltern or supine,
Untouchable without powers,
Remarkable without a mark.

In my tangibility,
In my humanity,
With my thoughts and desires,

I am the sorry opposite of my shadow.

January 13th . . . Again

The dark realm
Of unconditional love
Calls its young again;
Gathers the wind
With powerful hands,
And imprisons the son
Who will never be
Able but to collapse
Back in there, again—
Before the world,
Before the warm sun,
Before other women,
And before the eye
Splits the helpless 'I.'
I am Jewish, because
Of you, and I cry.
I am Christian, because
Of you, and I cry.
I am Muslim, because
Of you, and I cry.
I am nobody at all,
And I am enjoying it,
In spite of the pain.

Your saliva on that boy's
Soft and green little cheek
Removed the black stain
Of the school's playground,
And took its place—
Firmly, finally, and forever.

The Perfectionist

The Perfectionist
Claims be a god.
Once he sees
The dark stain
On his own
Alabaster skin,
He sees God
In the very spot
Of imperfection.
He becomes confused—
Who is God?
And why He loves
To appear
Only in the darkest,
The tiniest,
The dirtiest,
little places?
He sees
That the Perfectionist
Can only be so
When He identifies
With His imperfections.

Old Prostitutes

They just like the generosity
Of the drunken man
Who does not judge them—
Who is not sober enough
To give either love
Or even advice
In the cloak of the wise.

They just like the vulnerability—
The weakness of a man
Who reminds them
Of babies young enough
To demand love
As a natural right—
To own the world—

To be in unity
With the light
And the night—
To still be able to see them
As lovers and mothers,
No matter how haggard
They look;

No matter how raddled
They are—
How hollow-eyed—
Emaciated by life and love
And the long lost luster
That bewitched
So many others.

Solitary Figure

Thank you," she said,
"Free Palestine!"
I kissed her hand—
"The honour is mine."

A single soul
In a sea of strollers—
She's probably regarded
As a mad woman
By the busy people
Rushing by her frail figure.

Who thinks about Palestine
In a city like this one?
Who dares the smallest sign
Of solidarity with Palestine?

I took off my mask
For the precious picture.
She said: "I must keep mine
To protect myself
From the Zionists."
I wonder what she meant.
But she did manage to put
A caring smile on some faces.

The moment the prostitution
Of the world seems complete,
One 'crazy woman' decides
To put her hands in the fire
Of obsolete honour,
Committing social suicide,
And embarrassing us
To the point of wetting
Our expensive HK pants.

Saint

Are you proud now that you're reduced to this ink on paper?
It's glorious, I guess, like dying of too much wine.
But what about those bodies? What were they created for?
Oh, are you going to do the holy saint again?
When did saints ever have those eyes and that hair?
When did saints play with hearts
Just by showing up without saying anything?
When did saints inspire sinning just by being too beautiful?
Where was I when you decided to be a saint?
I guess it was my mistake; I should have been there,
I should have saved you from sainthood.
I should have saved you from the saints' God.

Unaccepted

It is only after the third glass of red
Or the fifth green bottle
That thoughts start to pop up.
When I am old and no longer able
To drink, what then? I always wondered.
Back to intellectual writing, I guess?
So will it be going from mind
To soul and then back to mind?
Why can't I give up both and become accepted?
Well, I guess some of us aren't made to be accepted;
Some are destined to disturb,
To stir the stagnant waters and
Let out the stench that underpins
Almost everything we do and say.
Some are just destined to get drunk
On whatever they love.
Not everyone can follow Baudelaire's advice;
It is not easy to get drunk with what you love.
It is easier to be accepted—and just live.

Lost Time

Look at the days you lost,
Look at the hours you wasted
With no song,
With no dance,
With no guts.

Consider every time lost,
In which you have not
Surrendered yourself
At least once
To the readers of these words.

Look at yourself,
O, Self,
And despair
Over the moments of no food,
No drink, and no air.

Simple Beings

If you have enough courage
To ask them directly,
They would tell you
That the truth
Is not a mythical beast;
That they are, in fact,
Satisfied with the least,
They just want the world
To go on as usual—
Intact.

We overestimate
Their ambitions,
When all they want is
Someone who's simply
Available;
They don't even mind
Being betrayed
From time to time;
They are just concerned
With being left alone;

They cannot be lonely;
They become dangerous
When they are lonely.

We must attend properly
To these delicate gregarious
Simple beings.

Without You

I am starting this brand new
Writing project without you.
Without your face and your smile,
Without your beautiful legs and arms,
And all the charms
That stood between my pen
And this overly receptive paper.

It is only logical that I should be less
Distracted now, I guess.
For I'm not thinking about you
While I am writing this poem.
I am not thinking about your beauty,
I am not thinking about your body,
I am not thinking how every rhyme
Rhymes with your sometimes-pouting lips.
No, no, I do not have your nipples or your hips
On my mind anymore, I am a prolific poet,
Who can write, in any circumstance—
In your presence, or in your absence.

I do not know why I am getting angry,
I must be feeling hungry.
Anyway, I just wanted to say
That I am not thinking about you
While writing this poem—
Obviously.

Wine, Woman, and Pen

Excuse me,
But, my vision is impaired
By this wine.

I cannot
See you the way
You want me to—

I can only write it.

Don't be surprised;
The red liquid
Makes people more beautiful
Than they actually are.

And too much beauty
Calls for literature—
Not reality.

My eyes are enjoying you
But my pen happens to be
In control
When I have none.

Red Wine Discourse

Well, my friend,
It's impossible to write
When the powerful
Are too powerful
And the weak
Are too weak;

When the powerful
Think they're weak,
And the weak think
They're invincible;

When the victimizer
And the victimized
Look strangely alike;

When the sage and the sane
Are nobodies in between.

It's impossible to write,

And even if I write,
How to face those eyes,
Be able to move that
Heavy tongue and recite?

Women and the Muslim Tradition

Why don't we just kill them
If they're all that trouble?
If they're the reason why
We were kicked out of heaven
And the great grandmother
Was that serpent,

And they're infatuation
From head to toe,
And dangerous pits where
We're not supposed to fall
Yet fall into all the time
And enjoy being there,

Why don't we just rid the world
Of those dangerous creatures?
If we have to hide them
Because our eyes were built
To gaze upon those curves,
Why don't we just exterminate

Them, or, if we're brave enough,
Blind ourselves Oedipus style?
Covering them obviously doesn't work;
We still fantasize about what's
Under the cover—even more.
Oh, I see it now—

Those men of God
Are far more intelligent than we think;
They created a religion that revolves
Around woman out of lust,
So that men can enjoy her
More as a sin—a forbidden object

And still vilify her as the serpent—
That irresistible serpent
With the S shaped body
That man's God created, loved, hated,
Demonized, idolized, and fucked
All at once.

Gaza

Make no mistake!
There will be
No mourning;
No earth to earth,
Ashes to ashes,
Dust to dust.
There will be
No prayers,
and no libations.
Mark this:
Since you made
A night too murky
To overcome,
There will be
No morning,
No new sun,
And no memory—
Only a present,
At a precipice,
Where no one
Is safe, for a long
Long time to come.

You and I

The problem is
I am no one else—
Just me.

And, I can't be
Anyone else,
So, I just have to be,

And you—
Well, I am sorry;
You'll have to suffer me.

Guilt

I have nothing to do with it, I think,
I should have nothing to do with it—
The children's blood casually spilt
In defiant Gaza by the Nazi Zionist.
But why does the wine taste like blood?
Oh God, why does it taste like blood?
Is it a color effect? Too much of it
Shown on screens that it seeps through
And colors the world? Or is it guilt?
Guilt—the very word makes me tremble;
The very thought of any connection;
And yet the more frightening thought
Of disconnection—
Here I am, children of great misfortune,
Sipping red wine and thinking that
It tastes like blood—
In other words, living, let alone, writing about it;
Writing about your blood in my glass
Turning into broken glass in my blood.

The Problem

The problem is that
She has always thought
I'm just too serious for her—
No fun, no petty talk,
Nothing like a simple walk
In the garden of lovers
Who don't care about
Anything but their little pleasure.

The problem is that
She could never figure me out
For what I really am—
Just a man
Who enjoys beer and women;
Just a man who writes
Posthumously—
After getting drunk,
After the body is
Sufficiently deadened,
And after fantasizing
About her silent house
In terms of other women
Who just fill in in her place.

The problem is that
She couldn't ever imagine
That art may not be that serious;
It is only a little compensation
For our constant need
To consume people,
Not art, but people—
Their bodies and their lives.
She just couldn't understand
That this is the real desire
Of everybody
Without exception.

The problem is that
She couldn't ever see
That I am not a prophet.
I am not even a poet.
I am not anything at all
But a man who just
Wanted her body.

The problem is that
She saw in me much more than me,
And, may be,
It scared her to death
To imagine that in truth
I am just another man
Who is pretending to be
Someone else
Just to get to those nipples
And chew them.

One of us is mistaken

If you think that I still love you, you're mistaken.
I love this wine, this pen, and this paper,
More than anyone or anything now.
If you think that you are more important
Than giving birth to these lines that
Will probably be read by no one but me,
You're mistaken.
These lines are far more important than your love—
Even if no one will ever care to read them.
If you think that you still inspire these lines,
You're mistaken—
They're inspired by this red Bordeaux
Which somehow seems to argue
That it is, in reality, nothing but you.

Liquid

There's no doubt about it; it's been proven empirically;
The red liquid, always, leads to writing.
Those green bottles often lead to writing too.
Being away from people, always, leads to writing.
And as one grows up, he gets driven away from people,
He gets closer to the liquid that churns out literature.
"People are pointless," as the wise drunkard once said.

Lullaby

Children, wait for us
In the darkness of death!
We're on our way too,
Like all the things
That are to die.

The difference though
Is that you were lucky
Enough not to live long
And witness our collective
Conspiratorial cowardice.

Here's a lullaby
To help you sleep peacefully:

The gang of half-breeds
That held control for years
Through displaced shame and guilt
Is no longer believed

Except by half-breeds.

Recommended Readings, Films, and Operas

Adorno, Theodor W. *Aesthetic Theory*. Edited and Translated by Robert Hullot-Kentor. Minneapolis: University of Minnesota Press, 1998.

Baudelaire, Charles. *Baudelaire: Poems*. Translated by Richard Howard. New York: Everyman's Library, 1994.

Baudrillard, Jean. *America*. Translated by Chris Turner. London: Verso, 1988.

Benigni, Roberto. *La vita è bella*. Italy: Melampo Cinematografica, 1997.

Bukowski, Charles. *The Pleasures of the Damned: Selected Poems 1951–1993*. Edinburgh and London: Canongate, 2018

Cavafy, C.P. *Cavafy: Poems*. Edited and translated by Daniel Mendelsohn. New York: Everyman's Library, 2014.

Chow, Rey. "Rereading Mandarin Ducks and Butterflies: A Response to the 'Postmodern' Condition." *Cultural Critique* (Winter 1986–1987) 69–93. Minneapolis: University of Minnesota Press, 1986.

Debord, Guy. *The Society of the Spectacle*. Translated by Fredy Perlman. New York: Critical Editions, 2021.

Kafka, Franz. *The Complete Stories*. Edited by Nahum N. Glatzer, Foreword by John Updike. Translated by Mark Harman, Breon Mitchell, James Stern, Elisabeth Duckworth, Philip Boehm, Richard Winston and Clara Winston. Schocken,Germany: Penguin Random House, 2012.

Lacan, Jacques. *The Four Fundamental Concepts of Psycho-Analysis*. Edited by Jacques-Alain Miller. Translated by Alan Sheridan. Harmondsworth: Penguin, 1994.

Lawrence, D.H. *Studies in Classic American Literature*. Harmondsworth: Penguin, 1977.

Nietzsche, Friedrich. *Twilight of the Idols*. Translated by Richard Polt. Introduction by Tracy B. Strong. Indianapolis: Hackett, 1997.

Shakespeare, William. *Anthony and Cleopatra*. Edited by Michael Neill. Oxford: Oxford University Press, 2001.

Sontag, Susan. *Regarding the Pain of Others*. New York: Picador, Farrar, Straus and Giroux, 2003.

Sophocles. *Oedipus Rex*. Edited by Elizabeth Osborne. Translated by J.E. Thomas. Clayton, DE: Prestwick, 2004.

The Bible: Authorized King James Version with Apocrypha. Oxford: Oxford University Press, 1998.

The Holy Qur'aan. Translated by A. Yusuf Ali. Brentwood, MD: Amana Corp, 1983.

The Talmud. Translated by H. Polano. San Diego: The Book Tree, 2003.

Wagner, Richard. *Der Ring des Nibelungen*. New York: James Levine and the Metropolitan Opera Orchestra, 2006.

Wagner, Richard. *Tristan und Isolde*. UK: EMI Classics, 2006.